CHURCH MUSIC SOCIETY PUBLICATION: 023A
Hon. General Editor: Richard Lyne

for the Choir and Congregation of St. Mary's Church,

Saint Mary's Mass

Music by ANTHONY CÆSAR

Kyrie

Alternative version of Kyrie

Gloria

3

For you— a-lone are the Ho-ly One, you a-lone are the Lord,—

you a-lone are the Most High, Je-sus Christ, with the Ho-ly Spi-rit,

in the glo-ry of God— the Fa-ther. A - men. A - men.

Gospel Responses

Glo - ry to Christ— our Sa - viour.

Praise — to Christ — our Lord. —

Sanctus – Benedictus

Ho-ly, Ho-ly, Ho - ly Lord, God— of pow'r and

might, heav'n— and earth are full— of your glo - ry. Ho-san-na in the

high-est. Bless - ed is he who comes— in the name— of the

Lord. Ho-san - na in the high-est, Ho - san - na in the high - est.

Acclamations

Agnus Dei

Acknowledgment

The *Gloria*, the *Sanctus*, the *Benedictus* and the *Agnus Dei* from *The Order for Holy Communion Rite A* from the Alternative Service Book 1980 are © International Consultation on English Texts and are reproduced with permission of the Central Board of Finance of the Church of England.

ISBN 0-19-395363-3

Origination by Jeanne Fisher, Ludlow, Shropshire
Printed by Halstan & Co. Ltd., Amersham, Bucks

Pack of 10 copies
Not available separately

9 780193 953635